sundance
publishing

LITTLE RED
READERS

Super Sandwich

PETER SLOAN &
SHERYL SLOAN

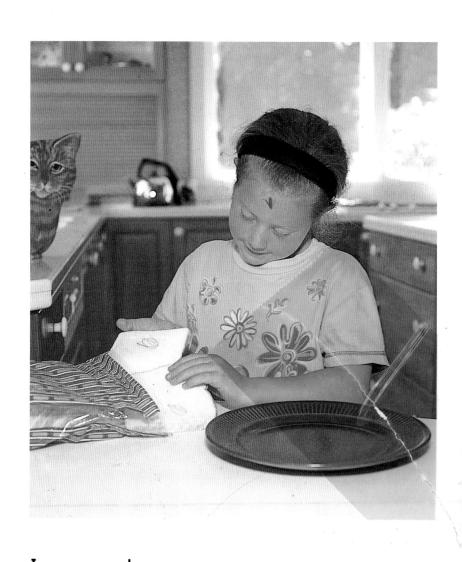

I was hungry,
so I made a sandwich.
I took out
two slices of bread.

2

I put two slices of ham
on one slice of bread.

I put some lettuce
on the ham.

I put some tomato
on the lettuce.

I put some cheese
on the tomato.

I put some mustard
on the cheese.

I put the other slice
of bread on top.
I couldn't get
my super sandwich
into my mouth.

8